READY, SET, CODE!

CODING with

ScratchJr

Álvaro Scrivano

Illustrated by Sue Downing

Lerner Publications ◆ Minneapolis

First American edition published in 2019 by Lerner Publishing Group, Inc.

First published in Great Britain in 2018 by Wayland
Copyright © Hodder and Stoughton, 2018
All rights reserved.

Editor: Sarah Silver
Design and illustrations: Collaborate

Lerner Publications Company
A division of Lerner Publishing Group, Inc.
241 First Avenue North
Minneapolis, MN 55401 USA

For reading levels and more information, look up
this title at www.lernerbooks.com.

Main body text set in Frutiger LT Pro 45 Light.
Typeface provided by Linotype AG.

Library of Congress Cataloging-in-Publication Data

Names: Scrivano, Álvaro, 1973– author. | Downing, Sue, 1964- illustrator.
Title: Coding with ScratchJr / Álvaro Scrivano ; [illustrator] Sue Downing.
Description: Minneapolis : Lerner Publications, [2019] | Series: Ready, set, code! "First published in Great Britain in 2018 by Wayland, Copyright, Hodder and Stoughton, 2018." | Audience: Ages 7–11. | Audience: Grades 4 to 6. | Includes bibliographical references and index.
Identifiers: LCCN 2018030527 (print) | LCCN 2018032651 (ebook) | ISBN 9781541543041 (eb pdf) | ISBN 9781541538757 (lb : alk. paper) | ISBN 9781541546684 (pb : alk. paper)
Subjects: LCSH: Scratch (Computer program language)—Juvenile literature. | Computer programming—Juvenile literature.
Classification: LCC QA76.73.S345 (ebook) | LCC QA76.73.S345 S37 2019 (print) | DDC 005.13/3—dc23

LC record available at https://lccn.loc.gov/2018030527

Printed in China
1-45058-35885-7/9/2018

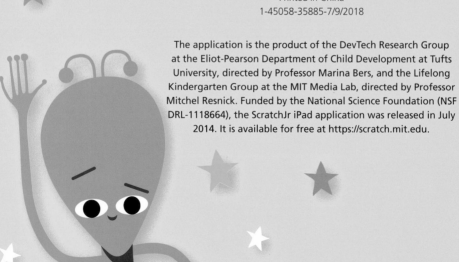

The application is the product of the DevTech Research Group at the Eliot-Pearson Department of Child Development at Tufts University, directed by Professor Marina Bers, and the Lifelong Kindergarten Group at the MIT Media Lab, directed by Professor Mitchel Resnick. Funded by the National Science Foundation (NSF DRL-1118664), the ScratchJr iPad application was released in July 2014. It is available for free at https://scratch.mit.edu.

Contents

Make sure you are always with an adult when you download applications or files from the internet.

What Is ScratchJr?

ScratchJr is a programming language. It allows you to drag and combine code blocks to make interactive stories, games, and animations. Once you have tried the activities in this book, you will be able to use many different features in ScratchJr to create and make just about anything you want!

Note to parents:

ScratchJr runs on both iPads and Android tablets. To use ScratchJr you need to open the App Store on your iPad or Google Play on your Android tablet. Search for ScratchJr. Select "Get" to download the app from the App Store or "Install" to download from Google Play. For more information about the requirements for running ScratchJr, visit: www.scratchjr.org/about/faq.

The projects in this book need access to the device camera and microphone. To enable them, go to Settings>Privacy>Camera.

ScratchJr interface

When you open a new project in ScratchJr, you will see this home page. Here are some details about all the features you can see.

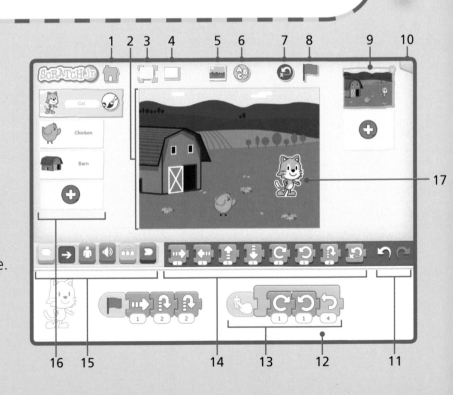

1 Save: Save the current project and exit to the home page.

2 Stage: This is where the action takes place in the project. To delete a character on the stage, press and hold the character.

3 Presentation Mode: Expand the stage to full screen.

4 Grid: Turn the x-y coordinate grid on and off.

5 Background: Select or create a background image for the stage.

6 Add Text: Write titles and labels on the stage.

7 Reset Characters: Reset all characters to their starting positions on the stage.

8 Green Flag: Start all programming scripts that begin with a "Start on Green Flag" block by tapping here.

9 Pages: Select the pages in your project, or tap the plus sign to add a new page. Each page has its own set of characters and a background. To delete a page, press and hold it. To reorder pages, drag them to new positions.

10 Project Information: Change the title of the project and see when the project was created.

11 Undo and Redo: If you make a mistake, tap the left arrow to go back. Tap the right arrow to go forward.

12 Programming Area: This is where you connect programming blocks to create scripts.

13 Programming Script: Snap blocks together to make a programming script, telling the character what to do. Tap anywhere on a script to make it run. To delete a block or script, drag it outside the programming area. To copy a block or script from one character to another, drag it on to the character's thumbnail.

14 Blocks Panel: This is the menu of programming blocks. Drag a block into the programming area, then tap on it to see what it does.

15 Block Categories: This is where you can select a category of programming blocks: triggering (yellow), motion (blue), looks (purple), sounds (green), control (orange), and end (red) blocks.

16 Characters: Choose the characters in your project or tap the plus sign to add a new one. Once a character is selected, you can edit its scripts, tap its name to rename it, or tap the paintbrush to edit its image. To delete a character, press and hold it. To copy a character to another page, drag it to the page thumbnail.

17 Felix: Felix is the name of the orange cat that you see at the start of every new project. You can use Felix in your project or delete him and add a new character.

MOON LANDING

ARE YOU READY TO GO TO THE MOON?

READY >>

In this project you are going to program an animation with you as an astronaut walking on the moon. But before you start, you will have to follow a few simple steps to get ready.

1 GETTING STARTED

Find the ScratchJr app on your device and tap on it to open it. Tap on the home button. To start a new project, tap on the plus sign.

Did you know?

On April 12, 1961, a Russian cosmonaut named Yuri Gagarin became the first person to orbit Earth.

SET

Before you start coding you need to set up the scene where your animation will take place and add characters to animate.

2 ADD A BACKGROUND

To choose a suitable backdrop for your animation, tap the background button at the top of the screen to go to the background library.

Find the moon landscape and tap on it twice to select it. The moon background will appear. This is where your animation will take place.

3 DELETE A CHARACTER

If you want to animate a different character, you need to delete Felix first. To delete Felix, find him on the left-hand side of your screen. Tap and hold until you see a red X. Tap on the X to delete Felix.

4 ADD A CHARACTER

All the characters are listed on the left of your screen. To add a new one, tap the add button:

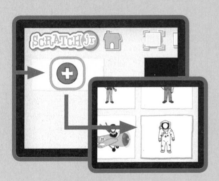

Scroll through the character library until you find the astronaut. When you find it, tap it twice. It will appear on the background. Drag the astronaut and drop it on the right-hand side of the screen. This will be the character's starting position.

5 ADD YOUR PICTURE

You are going to add your own picture inside the astronaut helmet. Tap on the brush next to the astronaut character to edit it. Tap on the camera button and then tap inside the astronaut's helmet:

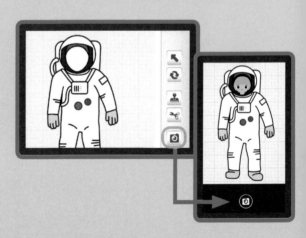

Now take a picture of yourself. Look excited! You are walking on the moon! Once you have taken the picture, tap the check mark symbol. You will see your picture inside the astronaut helmet.

CODE!

Now you are ready to make a program for your character. Use the colored blocks on the bottom left to locate the coding blocks that you need.

> **Wow! You're walking on the moon!**

Remember: the green flag will start your animation and the red button will stop it.

6 ANIMATE USING THE MOTION BLOCKS

To move the characters in your animation, you use the motion blocks. The motion blocks are blue and positioned on the left-hand side of the screen. The number underneath each block shows how many times the character will make a movement. First, let's make the astronaut walk and jump. Tap on the astronaut in the character list and add the following code:

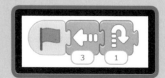

7 ANIMATE USING THE REPEAT BLOCK

The repeat block is used to repeat something lots of times, and is also known as a loop. You can use the repeat block to make the astronaut repeat the same movement.

Tap on the astronaut in the character list. To use the repeat block, insert the blocks you want to be repeated inside the repeat block, like this:

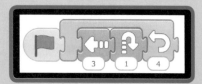

Tap on the green flag in the code or the green flag at the top of the page to test your animation.

Did you know?
Neil Armstrong became the first human ever to stand on the moon.

9

I like the sound of that!

8 ANIMATE USING SOUND

To add some sound to your animation, first tap on the astronaut and then tap on the speaker button.

Tap on the microphone and you will see a square box in the middle of the screen. Tap on the red button and record your voice saying: "Yay! I've landed on the moon!"

Then tap the check mark symbol to add your voice to the animation. Add the green microphone to the code. Tap on the green flag to test your animation.

9 ADD CHARACTERS TO YOUR PROGRAM

You can add more characters and animate them too. Scroll down through the character library until you see a star character.

Tap on the star twice to add it to your project. Drag the star and drop it on the top left-hand corner. You can change the color and shape of your star by going to character edit. For more guidance on how to change your character's appearance, see step 3 on page 25.

To make the star shine in the background, tap on the star and add the following code:

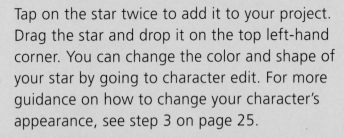

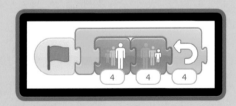

MAKE A CHARACTER DISAPPEAR

You can also make a star shoot across your background! To do this, scroll through the character library until you see a shooting star character. Tap on the shooting star twice to add it to your animation. Drag the shooting star and drop it on the left-hand side below the star.

To make the shooting star get a little bigger and then disappear, add the following code to it:

Tap the green flag to test your animation.

TROUBLESHOOTING
Did the shooting star reappear on the left-hand side of the scene at the end of the animation? That's because it started somewhere in the middle of the screen. To solve this problem, you need to ensure the shooting star is placed on the left, under the star at the beginning of the animation.

CHALLENGE

Use what you've learned in this project to create your own space animation. Change the background, add different stars, and make the astronaut fly in space.

UNDER THE SEA

WOULD YOU LIKE TO EXPLORE THE DEEP BLUE SEA?

READY >>

In this project you are going to program an animation with you as a scuba diver exploring the deep blue sea. Let's get ready to dive!

1. GETTING STARTED

As you did in the previous project, you will have to find the ScratchJr app on your device. Tap on the home button. Press on the plus sign to start a new project.

Did you know?
Oceans cover nearly 71 percent of Earth's surface. They contain almost 98 percent of all the water on Earth.

This animation is going to be of a diver in the sea, so you need to choose a background that shows an underwater scene.

2 ADD A BACKGROUND

Tap the background button at the top of the screen to go to the background library.

Find the underwater background and tap it twice. Add the same background to a second screen as well—you will use this later on.

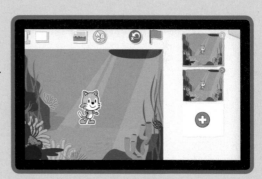

3

ADD CHARACTERS

Delete Felix and add new characters by tapping on the plus sign on the left-hand side of the screen.

For this animation you will need a whale and a scuba diver. As you scroll down the library, tap on a character and you will see its name on top of the screen.

Did you know?

There is one world ocean, but it is divided into five main areas: the Pacific, the Atlantic, the Indian, the Arctic, and the Southern or Antarctic.

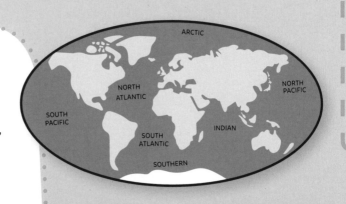

4

ADD YOUR PICTURE

You might have noticed that the diver has no face. Since you will be the explorer in this adventure, you need to take a picture of yourself to appear inside the diver.

Tap on the camera button and then tap inside the diver's helmet. Now take a picture of yourself and tap the check mark symbol. Your picture will appear inside the diver's helmet. You are now ready to explore the sea!

CODE! >>

Once you have the right background and characters, you can start programming your animation.

Remember: the green flag will start your animation and the red button will stop it.

5

SEQUENCING

In this step, you will animate the characters to do actions one after the other. This is called sequencing.

Tap on the diver in the character list and add a green flag and a purple speech block. Tap on the box below the bubble and type in "A whale!" Tap on the green flag to test the speech block.

BUILD A SEQUENCE

Add a color envelope from the yellow trigger blocks and change its color to blue by tapping on the triangle below. This color will send a trigger message to another character. Finally, add a red message to send the animation to the next screen (see page 20).

(see page 20)

The diver's code should look like this:

Tap on the whale and add the following code:

Instead of a green flag, there is a blue envelope in this code. This is to set up a sequence of events. The blue envelope in the diver's code will trigger the whale to move forward.

Did you know?
Whales are the largest animals that have ever lived on Earth. They are even bigger than the largest dinosaur was!

7

ADD A PROGRAM TO PAGE 2

Tap on the second page on the right-hand side and add the diver with your picture on it. Go back to the character page and tap on the diver.

8

MAKE A CHARACTER DISAPPEAR

Tap on the diver and add the following code:

In the speech bubble, type in, "That was amazing!"

Now go to page 1 and tap on the green flag to test your animation.

CHALLENGE

Use your knowledge about sequencing to make your animation more exciting. Add characters, such as a seahorse and a crab. Make them move along the page in different ways one after the other.

FINISH

I'm going to win!

TROUBLESHOOTING

It is sometimes difficult to calculate the place on the screen where the character will disappear.
To solve this, tap on the grid box button at the top of the screen (a red line will appear across the grid box) and you will see a coordinate grid on your screen. You can count how many squares your character will move before it disappears off the top or bottom of the screen.

The square in red is the position of the character

Grid box

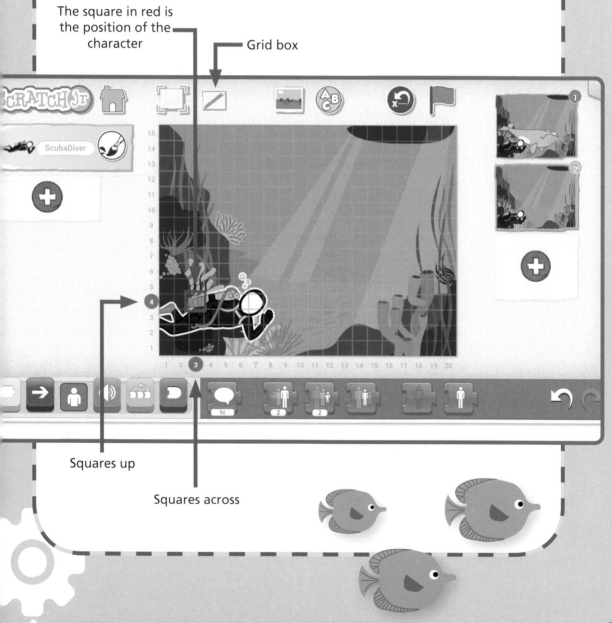

Squares up

Squares across

THE DRAGON, THE WIZARD, AND THE FAIRY

TELL THE STORY OF A DRAGON WHO WANTED TO SET A CASTLE ON FIRE.

READY »

In this project you are going to program an animation where a dragon is trying to destroy a castle, but a skillful wizard stops it.

1 **GETTING STARTED**
Find the ScratchJr app on your device. Tap on the home button. Press on the plus sign to start a new project.

Did you know?
Windsor Castle is the biggest castle in England. It is one of the three homes used by Queen Elizabeth II.

SET

Let's set the scene by adding a background and characters for the story.

2 ADD A BACKGROUND

Tap the background button at the top of the screen to go to the background library.

Find the farm background and tap it twice. Add the same background to two other pages as you will use them later on.

3

ADD CHARACTERS

Delete Felix from all three backgrounds and add new characters by tapping on the plus sign on the left-hand side of the screen.

For the first page of this animation, you will need a dragon and a castle. When you scroll down the library, tap on a character and you will see its name on top of the screen.

Did you know?

Prague Castle in the Czech Republic is the biggest castle in the world. It is 1,870 feet long and 430 feet wide!

4 PLACE THE CHARACTERS

Position the castle on the bottom right-hand corner of the page by dragging it from the center of the screen. Place the dragon above the castle. You are now ready to program your story!

CODE! ≫

Remember: the green flag will start your animation and the red button will stop it.

5 MAKE THE DRAGON FLY

Tap on the dragon in the character list and add the following code:

Press the green flag to test your animation.

If you tap on the red end blocks, you will notice that there is a block with a picture and a number 2 on the top right-hand corner. This block makes the animation continue on page 2. Add this red block to the dragon program to make the story continue on to the next page. It should look like this:

Did you know?

Segovia Castle in Spain is almost 1,000 years old and has been the home to many Spanish kings and queens.

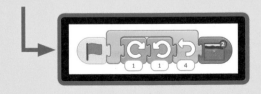

6 SEQUENCING THE ANIMATION

Add the dragon, the castle, and the wizard to page 2. Add the same code for the dragon as in the previous step without the red block.

You will now make the dragon interact with the wizard. Tap on the dragon. Add two send message blocks (colored envelopes) to the dragon's code to trigger an action on the wizard.

Tap on the wizard and add the following code. We have used "Abracadabra!" for this project, but you can use any magical word you want.

Ensure you choose the same color for the send message blocks as for the dragon. The orange block in the dragon code will make the wizard speak. The red block in the wizard will make the dragon disappear.

Add a red block at the end of the dragon program to send the animation to page 3.

 7

ADD MORE CHARACTERS

Add the castle, the wizard, and the fairy to page 3. Place the castle in the bottom right-hand corner as in the previous page.

8

ANIMATE USING CONTROL BLOCKS

You will use the wait block for the wizard. Tap on the wizard and add the following code:

The wait block will give time for the fairy character to appear on the screen.

Abracadabra!

9

ADD SPEED TO YOUR ANIMATION

Tap on the fairy and add the following code:

The speed block will give time for the fairy to appear on the screen after the wizard disappears.

Now, tap on the green flag to test your animation.

TROUBLESHOOTING

You can change the speed of an action if it is not happening at the right time. In the speed control block, click on the triangle below. You will find three speed levels:

 = slow

 = medium

 = fast

Adjust the speed of the fairy and the wizard.

CHALLENGE

Add sound to the dragon and the fairy to make your animation more exciting. Click on the play recorded sound block. Record your sound and add it to each character.

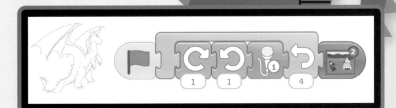

LET'S PLAY BASKETBALL!

CREATE AN ANIMATION ABOUT A CAT THAT PLAYS BASKETBALL.

READY >

The cat on this animation is a very skillful basketball player. He can bounce the ball, jump, shoot to the hoop, and score!

1

GETTING STARTED
As you did in the previous projects, you will have to find the ScratchJr app on your device. Tap on the home button. Press on the plus sign to start a new project.

Did you know?
Basketball was created in the US by a professor named Dr. James Naismith in 1891. The first basketball games had nine players on each team and used a soccer ball.

SET

Now you can choose a background and get your basketball player ready for the animation.

2 CHANGING THE CHARACTER

Delete Felix and then tap on the plus sign to add a new character.

In the library find the "Cat Walking" character and tap on the brush to edit it.

3

CHANGING THE CHARACTER'S APPEARANCE

Let's make the cat look like a basketball player.

A Change its color by clicking on the bucket on the bottom right-hand side.

B Choose a color and then tap on the cat.

C Add a headband by tapping the line at the top left corner of the screen.

D Choose the thickest line at the bottom and choose a color as you did in Step B. Draw the headband.

E Delete "Cat Walking" and type in "Basketball Player."

F This character is now added to the library. Tap on the top right-hand corner of the screen to add the basketball player to page 1.

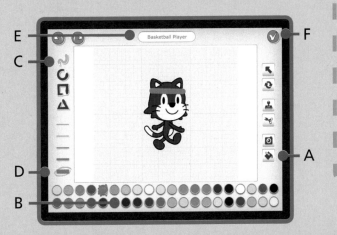

4 ADD AN OBJECT

The cat needs a ball to play basketball. Add a basketball from the library to page 1.

5 ADD A BACKGROUND

Tap the background button at the top of the screen to go to the background library.

Find the gym background and tap it twice. Add the same background to a second page.

Drag the basketball player and the ball and position them in the middle of the court. Drag the player and place its right hand in front of the ball to make it look like they are bouncing it.

Did you know?

Sheryl Swoopes became the first-ever player to be signed by the WNBA (Women's National Basketball Association) in their first season in 1997. She played for the Houston Comets.

ou now have the background and characters to
art programming your basketball animation.

6

RESIZE CHARACTER

Let's make the basketball smaller
to make it fit better with the cat's
size. Tap on the ball and copy the
following code:

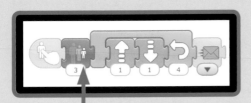

This block will make the
ball smaller. The bigger
the number, the smaller
the ball will become.

This code will make
the animation start
when you tap on the
basketball. The orange
envelope at the end
will send a message to
the cat to shoot at the
hoop. This is called a
trigger message. Tap on
the basketball on page 1
to test your animation.

**I think I need a
smaller size.**

Did you know?
Kareem Abdul-Jabbar is
the NBA's top scorer of
all time. He scored 38,387
points throughout his
career!

7 USING A TRIGGER MESSAGE

After bouncing the ball, the cat will have a shot at the hoop. Tap on the cat and add the following code:

You might have noticed that this program starts with an orange envelope. This is because the orange envelope in the ball's program triggers an action on the cat.

Tap on the ball again and add the following blocks to the program you did in Step 6.

The red block at the end will make the animation move to page 2:

Tap on page 2 and add the basketball player character and the basketball. Place the ball under the hoop and the basketball player in the middle of the court.

8 RESIZING CHARACTERS AND SEQUENCING

Tap on the basketball and add the following code:

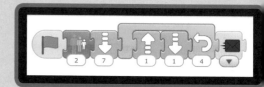

Finally, tap on the cat and add the following program:

Now, tap on the basketball on page 1 to show the whole animation.

1, 2, 3, 4 sequencing!

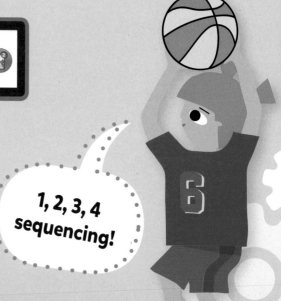

Did you know?

Men's basketball was first played in the Olympics in 1936 and women's basketball became an Olympic sport in 1976.

CHALLENGE

Use the purple looks blocks to add a speech bubble to the player saying, "Yes!" after they score.

Can you make the player dribble the ball? Using the blue motion blocks, try to make the player dribble with the ball.

GLOSSARY

Animation
Something that moves around on screen and looks like it has come to life

App (Application)
A self-contained program that performs a specific function for end-users

Character
A person or animal in a story

Code
A language for expressing information and instructions that can be understood by a computer

Coordinate
A set of numbers used to locate a point on a line, map, or grid

Interact
Communicate or spend time with something

Interface
The way a computer program looks on screen; for example, the layout of the screen and the menus

Library
A collection of characters and backgrounds

Loop
A series of instructions that is repeated until a condition to end it is met

Orbit
A repeated movement around an object, such as the moon orbiting Earth

Program
A set of instructions in code that a computer follows

Sequence
The order in which instructions are given to the computer

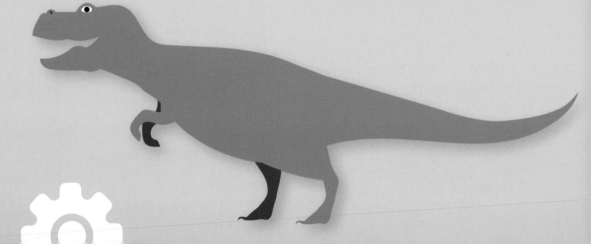

FURTHER INFORMATION

BOOKS

The Official ScratchJr Book by Marina Umaschi Bers and Mitchel Resnick (No Scratch Press, 2015)

Generation Code: I'm an Advanced Scratch Coder by Max Wainewright (Wayland, 2017)

WEBSITES

http://scratchjr.org

https://scratch.mit.edu

INTERNET SAFETY

The internet is a great resource that helps you connect, communicate, and be creative.

However, you need to stay safe online. Always remember:

1. If you see anything online which makes you feel uncomfortable or unhappy, tell a grown up straight away.

2. Never share your personal information, such as your full name, address, or date of birth, with anybody online.

3. Remember that people online may not always be who they say they are. Never share anything with people online unless you are sure you know who they are.

Note to parents
It is advisable to:

- Use filtering software to block unwanted content

- Familiarize yourself with the privacy settings of your device

- Set up passwords to protect personal information.

INDEX